April 2015

D1742268

Sarah,

enjoy!

A Swan in Flight

A Collection of Poems

Bernadette McCarrick

Bernadette McCarrick

Boland Press

First published in 2015
Copyright © Bernadette McCarrick

Boland Press
Grove Mill
Hollyfort
Co. Wexford
http://bolandpress.blogspot.com

A CIP catalogue record for this book
is available from the British Library

ISBN: 978-1-907855-10-8

Cover photograph by Geraint Parfitt
Cover design by Boland Press

Printed in Ireland by
SPRINT-Print

For my mother Brigid

Acknowledgement is given to the following publications where some of these poems, or versions of them, have appeared:

Women's Work IX (published by The Works, Wexford, 1998)
Review for Religious, Vol 58, No. 1 (Jan-Feb 1999) St. Louis Missouri, USA
Cistercian Studies Quarterly, Vol 34.4, (1999) Salt Lake City Utah, USA
The Mayo Anthology 5, (1998) Mayo Co. Council.

A poem begins as a lump in the throat.
Robert Frost

Bernadette McCarrick was born in County Sligo. Her poems have been published in Ireland and USA, and broadcast on Ireland's Mid-West radio. She has won several awards for her poems and, in 2007, was short-listed for the Hennessy Literary Award for emerging poets. She was poetry editor for the Cistercian Studies Quarterly for 2 years.

A Swan in Flight is the poet's second collection following 'My Father's Barn' (2009).

Email: myfathersbarn@gmail.com

Contents

Poems to Preserve Things

I write poems to preserve things . . .
both for myself and for others.
Philip Larkin

Summer Mornings
after Nikki Giovanni

I always liked them best.

You could go out barefoot
on the wet grass

to feed your pet lamb
at the cow-house gate

pick up the fresh
eggs in the hen-house

and have your mother
make French toast for breakfast

before walking the almost mile
to school.

Rites of Passage

I

In Carnaleck school
the wooden bench sat two
or three in a pinch.

The inkwell
a white bucket
an inch in diameter

and full of black ink
was housed
in a hole in the middle

of a small brass bed
the brass lid of which
slid open and shut

under the pressure
of your hand. I gripped
the wood-handled pen

dipped the long nib
placed the blotting-paper
and began.

II

The transition to the use of ink
gave us our first lessons
in the practice of delicacy.

The nib –
not to be dipped too deeply
or leaned upon unduly –

held the ink, then let it down
a few words at a time
of the passage we transcribed.

Exhausted, we scrawled our first
indelible signatures, and although
far from fluency, we had arrived.

III

On Friday afternoons
we chanted new words from tiny print
in the school paint-box. Shades
of colour like the names of foreign cities
sang on our tongues: Sienna
Cobalt, Indigo, Crimson,
Magenta, Ochre, Umber, Vermillion.

We mixed them with authority
on the inside of our paint-box lids

palettes of yellows, blues, reds
hues of green and purple
we'd never seen before.

We darkened, lightened, tinted
our skies, our fields, our bogs
brightened our chimneyed houses
their gated gardens, their front doors.

We left untouched
small pentagons pencilled in
for gables of white-washed cottages
in the distance
awaiting their russet roofs
half hidden by the trees.

In my Grandfather's House

there were vinyl-covered floors
upstairs
and soft feather-beds.

Downstairs
on a kitchen table with formica top
a pink translucent vase of sweet pea
was placed. In lace-curtained summer

afternoons I went with Grandad
on the horse-drawn dray
to collect his creamery-cans
at the bottom of the road.

As we bumped our way
across the field
I clutched at his braces for balance.

Kathleen O'Hara

The woman of the house
had strong metal tongs
long enough to manage fire, to move it
to other hearths or houses
if the need arose.

The woman of the kitchen
placed red-hot coals
on huge pot-oven lids
to crisp the bacon, to bake
the crusty soda-bread for tea.

The woman of the fireplace
stoked by day and raked at night,
trawled the morning ashes
for the embers of yesterday
to set smoke rising early
from her square white chimney.

A Girl Called Katney

Kate McCarrick
Aunt Kate to us
Mrs McNulty to everyone else

I met you only once –
on a Sunday afternoon
in your house in Bella.

You came down from the room
and shakingly pressed
a shilling in my hand.

This was long before
I heard my father say
that your girlhood name was Katney

a name so beautifully coined
by which you were affectionately known
and now are still remembered.

Horseshoe Nails
for Frank

Blackened, fashioned
by the artist
into two musicians
mounted on an iron plinth
a stage for flute and fiddle:
Harry
James
Frank

Your father
his father
yourself
keeping alive
music as old as the blacksmith
in his ringing forge
and the sparks that flew
from shoes of horses you once knew.

A Penny's Worth
i.m. Frank Henry

Once I knew a man who changed
the lock on his front door
which left an open circle
in the lovely wood. So he sealed it
with a penny from his pocket.

The penny did the job
to such perfection that the man
polished it until it shone
with all the coppery colours
of the setting sun and harvest moon.

On summer evenings from then on
the penny winked and glinted
from the confines of its home
embedded roundly in the door, filling
the man's heart time and time again

with the pure pleasure of knowing
that never had a coin been put
to such good use, and yes, of course
that *The Hen-and-Chickens*, as he put it,
are nice for the Country House.

Two Poems
after William Carlos Williams

Confession I

I've been wearing
the new wellingtons
you'd carefully hidden away

before you left.
You probably intended
to wear them

out in the fields
on your return
at the end of term.

Forgive me.
my own were
so ugly

and simply
too smelly
to wear anymore.

Confession II

Something happened
to the Sports Section
of today's Irish Times.

I knew you were looking
forward to it when
you got home from work.

Forgive me.
It's just that I didn't check
and I used it to stuff my shoes.

They needed drying out
I got so drenched
on my way from the shop.

A Surprise in the Post

Mother
did you know
you were before your time?

Take that early summer morning
in nineteen eighty-two
when you walked out
and set your tape-recorder
on the pier at the front gate –

there was no Dawn Chorus
on the radio then.

You sent me the cassette.
Perhaps I'd written home
and said, *Here in Missouri*
the birds are very colourful
but they don't sing at all.

You were always so good
at reading between the lines.

By the Way

A rusted bed-frame
a gate
of sorts.

Crossing the bridge
above the motorway
a herd of friesians.

The moon
like a dog
followed us everywhere.

In an old felt hat
the cat
had kittens.

Understatements
for John

In his room of light
the tailor finishes each jacket
to perfection.
Some have linings
to tantalize the eye

and on occasion
when he wears one
slivers of colour
flicker at the cuff –
turquoise, saffron
cornflower blue enough

to turn us into birdwatchers
for whole evenings at a time
leaving us longing for another
sighting of the kingfisher

and waiting for the redwing
to take flight again
to give us just one more
glimpse of the scarlet
under his jet-black wing.

The Curate's Trees

I planted four trees
in the churchyard, he said.
My four favourite trees
four mountain ash:

one for its winter shapeliness
one for its filigree of leaf
one for its delicate twigs
one for its berries of red.

I planted those four trees
to be looking at, he said.
My four favourite trees.
Four mountain ash.

Cloud-Dogs
for Oscar

In the stone-walled fields
of the west of Ireland
he sees them for the first time –
animals walking, limping
on short thin legs
some kneeling as they graze.

He climbs a gate
to watch them gathering
into a woollen crowd
moving fluidly through a gap
and scattering up a hill
away from him.

Now he is Adam
in the Garden of Eden
charged with naming
the creatures of the earth
and as he searches
the small treasury of his words
he finds a name for them and points

Cloud-dogs, Daddy! Cloud-dogs!

There is a Want

within
that has no form
no name.

It comes unbidden
asking to be written
down   it struggles up
through blockages
of mulch and stone

trickling out at last
it overflows   becomes a stream
all hum and rush
goes underground again
reappears   sings
tumbles over everything
cuts a path to run in

skirting nothing   carves
a bed to lie in
deepens   widens to a river
foams and flows arriving in a sweep
fresh-water full of itself
at the salty salty sea.

During Housework

I know you were ironing the shirts
when I arrived unannounced
and that I insisted upon
being scribbled down without delay.

Forgive me for persisting
under the collar like that
for hissing at you the whole way
up the sleeves
Strike now while the iron is hot!

I wanted nothing more
than to be buttoned to a finish
to be allowed to rest at last
and folded into the stack
with all the others
still warm, crisp
and faintly fragrant to the touch.

Late and Early

Early commuters
grind to a halt
for swans.

Morning drops her child
late at the school door
Any chance of a kiss?

Magnolia blossoms
their open cups full
of late snow.

No rooster crowed
this dawn
tail-feathers instead.

Holiday's End

Mid November in Marbella –
the last of languid days
and of the tideless bluestone sea
to call our own.

Soon we'll be at home
with the hum of ordinary
daily tasks, exchanging
one per pleasure we had here.

We probably won't mind
muffling up against the salt wind
at Skerries where the sea is
tidal and moody as the weather.

Our bones are soaked in the cures
of the sun-in-the-south-of-Spain
so that winter in Ireland
won't seem to last so long.

That's what we tell ourselves
as we head home again.

To Walk in my Native Place

is to cross four bridges
in the first mile down the road
from the house where I was born.

It is to pass the houses
of neighbours who are gone,
to speak their names
into the overgrowth
of their lost gardens.

On a summer evening
it is to know by heart again
the contours of the Ox Mountains
making a place for the sun to set in.

But recently it was to stop and wait
for Seery's flock of sheep to cross
the road after their dipping
to watch the sheepdogs crouch
nipping at their heels to hurry them
while grown lambs were crying
in the chaos to their lost mother
Where am I?
Where are you?
Answer me!

The Dearest Freshness

There lives the dearest freshness
deep down things.

Gerard Manley Hopkins

The Skylark

After her sky-blue
soaring song

she

drops

like

a

stone

into her bog-cotton
heather-hidden nest.

First Calf

A springing heifer
knowing nothing of the pain to come
seeks a place to calve alone.

She has only her animal self
to teach her when to push
consume the afterbirth

lick her newborn clean
nudge him to his feet until he
finds his first feed

before they rest together
in the long flowery morning
of a summer's grass.

Whin Honey

April has come.
Bend down
to the yellow
blossom of the whin

and risk the thorn
for the almond-and-coconut
aroma.
Let bees come.

Let them make honey for us
to heal the winter
lingering in lung and bone –

whin honey by the spoonful
so we can sip the sun.

Birds

Colours hop
in February's grey hedges
finches.

The redwing
a blackbird
until she took flight.

On a rain-soaked lawn
three herons
stab the darkness.

Reflected
in the glass table-top
wild geese in flight.

Riverscape

At Carrick the boat begins
to move through the silken waters
of the Shannon
and Body remembers the womb
in which she once was carried.

Moored at Drumshanbo
under a chip of moon
asleep on our narrow berths
Body remembers the cradle
in which she once was rocked and rocked.

We seem to float
all the way to Tarmonbarry
past swans resting
past herons rising out of reeds
past Rooskey
past cattle at their drinking-place
past sheep in fenceless fields
past families of moorhens
past caring
about who is holding up the sky
and keeping the world at spin.

Bog Colours Near Ballaghaderreen

This sweep of bog at Bockagh Hill
deserves a gold medal for its colours.
Countless shades have slipped
from the tawny wings of a cock pheasant
or from the brush
of a water-colour artist in the sky.

Rich and plentiful, they have pooled
on this wash of heath
browning the graceful grasses
in lovely accidents of randomness.

Yellows bordering on orange
become a subtle buff at every edge.

Reds and ambers, deepening to plum
paint those little low saplings
that have no name
and bog-cotton white
stitches the blanket hem.

Green moss and lichens
carpet acres of turf and
sinewed heather purples the peat-land
covering it with shelter
for woodcock, snipe and grouse.

Here on this ribbon of bog-road
where curlews cry
and teal and mallard
burst from darkening bog-holes
I stand cathedralled.

Ode to Water

Water my bath
my bowl
my cup

Water my ground
my shower
my crop

Water my thirst
my comfort
my well

Water my dam
my thundering
fall

Water my lake
my river
my fish

Water my tide
my ocean
my drop

Water my eye
my kidney
my birth

Water my table
my blessing
my life.

Rain

Shower by shower
August leaves us
mushrooms at our feet.

After wind and rain
it snowed
cherry blossoms.

Thunder shower over
the horse chestnut trees
continue to rain.

Floating
in a rain-water barrel
the full moon.

Twin Chrysanthemums

Five evenings ago
I plucked two small flowers
from the first frost of winter.

They keep me company
as they rest novembering
in their orange vase.

Their soft white faces touch
as faces touch
in a photograph.

Posing on their stems
in water five times changed
they are keeping their heads

above it, as only flowers can
when their ground
has been taken from under them.

Old Rosebushes

Sunny morning, late November
the ruthless gardener prunes
each rosebush back to level ground

with gloved hands
he places the severed branches
in a wheelbarrow with last summer

for the burning. Before they go
I want to kneel by the wheelbarrow
to thank those roses

for their lemon, red and cream
for bud and bloom and thorn
for every fallen petal

and the fragrance
they've bestowed on us since June.

A Hymn to Beauty

You are the orange flame
on the kingfisher's breast
and also the cool of his green
where the river is murmuring.

You are the clean white
of a swan at rest
and also the strong ship
of her body sailing.

You are the primrose
scarf that the blue tit
wears at his throat
and under his tender wings.

You are the dark gloss
of a blackbird
her brightness of eye
and also the song that she sings.

You are the long night
lit by a yellow moon
and also the mellow dawn
and the welcome heat of the sun.

You are the timid fawn
all beauty and heartbeat
newly born.
You are all grace and peace.

Summer 2014

This year
Ireland has had a summer
to heal all summers past –
the ones that drenched the land
and left cattle short of fodder.

This year
Ireland has had a summer
still septembering itself
in hazy mornings
in evenings with light breezes
and in honey-coloured light
the whole day in between.

This year
the last of summer is rinsing
through the oranges and yellows
of autumn leaves and berries
and the blackened thistles
their lost heads floating on the air.

This year
summer is stretching beyond
the equinox and slanting
its last drawn-out shadows
over the long-gathered
harvest in the grateful fields.

A Swan in Flight

This morning
in Drogheda
the tock-tock of her wings
in flight
over the flower-bedecked bridges of the Boyne
in mid air
low above our heads she passed
her wingspan almost brushing
the walls of buildings
she sailed the air between
up river and through town
she flew wherever
she was heading
unhurriedly
she was leaving
she flew wherever
down river and out of town
she sailed the air between
the walls of buildings
her wingspan almost brushing
low above our heads she passed
in mid air
over the flower-bedecked bridges of the Boyne
in flight
the tock-tock of her wings
in Drogheda
this morning.

Trees

Windswept at the roots
stunted trees lean
away from the sea.

Sixteen cedars
by the Carmelites' wall
one per nun within.

A dead poplar
pretending to be alive
stands straight and tall.

Though long dead
the day the elm tree was felled
it crashed like thunder.

Everything Changes

*Everything changes. You can make
a fresh start with your final breath.*
                              Bertold Brecht

Storm Damage

You slept right through the storm
until the rain came
drumming down heavily at the end.

There you were next day
sweeping up the berries
and the snapped-off twigs
of the rowan tree, humming
as you washed the windows
smelled the clean fresh air
and straightened up
the clothesline, unaware

that rain had seeped
into the attic in the night
and was already spreading
its damp stain in secret –
a thing that was to be
repeated storm by storm

until the day you noticed
signs of damage on a ceiling
and you knew then
what you had to do.

If you Write

rather than rant or fret
you'll get the names
of all the dreads that dog you.
You'll let them off the leash
to do their hectic things
in the safe wilderness
of the page on which you write.

Something you cannot name
will cause you to respond
to every unacknowledged thing
you've pocketed for years

and you will scrawl your way
through grief
your pencil a splinter of hurt
recounting your losses and regrets
until they circle you
like standing-stones
here in your own meadow
which you now may leave
or enter at your ease
by the marvellous new gate
you've hung there.

You can lean on it and breathe.

And when you read
what you have written down
you'll gather up the pieces
of what once took place
into the rounded bowl
of fresh understanding
and whole new insights
shimmering with light.

You'll face whatever comes.

Court Abbey
i.m. Harry McCarrick

I

One year on I stand at your grave
recalling how we lowered you
into the frost-hardened earth
lined with the moss
we plucked from the Ox Mountains,

how we sprinkled you
with prayers and holy water
dropping into your grave
twigs we had broken
from the beech tree near the house

and how we sang you
into your native soil
our Salve Regina faltering
over the ancient stones of Court Abbey.

II

All year long we kept returning
to continue our goodbyes
allowing them to mingle
with the three purples of heather
we planted on your grave.

III

Meanwhile
just to let you know
that yesterday a Christmas fall of snow
blanketed the roof of your barn

and that the red door and little window
waited patiently for you
all night under the stars.

The Following Easter

sauntering
in a town in Spain

lemon drops
in small sealed tins

glimpsed in a shop window
drew me in

across the threshold
the penny dropped

stopped me in my tracks.

He's gone.

A Sighting

I saw him crossing
at the traffic-lights today
a nimble man of eighty years
dressed in tweed and serge
and shod in leather boots
hurrying about his business.

His peaked cap shaded his eyes
from the blinding winter sun
and kept him from seeing me
here in the car
watching him in disbelief
waiting for the light to change.

On the Death of a Friend
i.m. E. W.

It is the evening
of your burial day.
The prayers
have all been chanted
the water of blessing
sprinkled

among the banked flowers
on your grave
ruffled by the breeze
I place my bouquet

as night comes down
I leave you by the light
of a huge white moon
close and low in the sky.

It is your lamp now.
It burns for you.

In Eidfjiord Norway

The stave church grounds
are beautifully kept.

Mown grass and walks
enhance the simple headstones

set in rows. Each one bears a name
Erik or Olaf, followed by

a star for birth, a cross for death
a single line of scripture

flowers planted in the earth
and here and there a wooden seat

where a visitor can sit to read
the story on one leaning stone:

July the twenty-third, nineteen forty-one
twins, a boy and a girl
three days old.

Placing Stones

I have placed a stone
in secret and with tears
for the Tooth Fairy
and one for Santa Claus
pleased that I could scrape
their names at least
on each stone's face
without assistance

I know where they
can still be found
smothered by nettles
and a confusion of briars.

I have placed more stones
along the way
in private ceremonies
for myths uncovered
for meanings long outgrown
each bearing its inscription
in neat calligraphy.

On the current ritual stone
I am preparing
to chisel *Certainty*
but so far have not found
a place to lay it down.

A Longing

Oh to be as sure-footed as you
my little white goat
in your flock of twenty
scampering over the rocky parts
of the mountains that tower
above the fjiords of Norway.

Of course I realize
that for my part
I was reared on the flat
bog-softened land
in the west of Ireland

and that its turf for me
as these rocks for you
is the measure of my acuity.

Promise

I picture them
one by one
the boats I've missed

sail-torn, wind-blown
salt-blasted, rope-worn
arriving intact
on the other shore.

The next boat
already stocked
and bobbing at her moorings

will not leave without me.

Paradox

Paradox reconciles all contradictions
                              PL Fermor

Flowering whitethorns
showing no wood
and full of the hum of bees
seem to reproach me
for feeling lost and empty
in the presence of such
fragrance and abundance
leaning down the final days of May.

What can I say?
Am I not a tree made wood
by my own winter?
Seasons which oppose are
two opposing goods
where envy may not enter
to deny a paradox its irony
its chance to play
the contradiction game.

Walking the Land

In this dream a whole new country
strange and full of promise opens up.
It is covered in a light
blanket of springtime snow
and I am walking there
with pleasure across inviting fields
I've never seen before.

The scene is changing
and now they are the fields
of Branchfield, Carrowmore
and Cashel North. I know
these farms and houses
these very hedgerows by the way
they're edging up
to the foot of Knocknashee.

The dream ends as I approach
the crossroads, and it dawns on me
in the waking light of day
that each new country holds the old
familiar territory of home.

A Nun Takes her Leave

There was a time
when there was no goodbye.

One by one
the pennies dropped –

the thuck-thuck of high heels
the night before
on the wooden floor of her cell.

So late a doorbell.

The sound of a car-engine
idling at the back gate at midnight.

Her vacant place at breakfast.
Each stunned face
staring at her empty chair.

Upstairs her room stripped bare.
Her mattress airing
by the open window.
Her blankets folded up.

Her name, her loveliness
her unhappiness of late
not to be spoken of
for fear of causing discontent.

A Chapel

By All Souls' Day that year
the best place he could pray
was sitting on a milking-stool
among the housed cows
on the monastery farm.

The animals' clouded breath
their bellies big with calf
brought him a certain comfort
for which he had no name.

By Advent he had found
his way again
the choice he had to make
becoming clearer by the day.

Christmas came with gifts
of inner strength and peace

Epiphany
with ways to say goodbye
to each of his companions
before he took his leave.

Transformation
for Kevin

To my great surprise
Prayer one day came to me
in the hospital chapel
asked me to leave
and go with her.

She walked me
down the long corridor
(her carriage was beautiful)
told me her name from now on
was not Desperation

but Courage. We walked
all the way to Intensive Care
without stopping. We knocked
and went in helping each other
with those difficult
plastic aprons
bracing ourselves for the moment
when we would ask
the nurse on duty our question

So, how are things today?

Suffrage
for Dorrie

An old leather-skinned man
has travelled three days to the township
from his home in the hills.
He has arrived at the polling-station.
He stands in the doorway.
This way, Sir . . .

The old man cannot stir, because
with his bare feet
swollen from walking
he must savour this doorway.
With his hands
thickened by seventy years
of work in the fields
he must caress this doorway.
He must close his eyes and sigh
and lean his whole voiceless life
into this doorway.
This way, Sir . . .

Solemnly he moves towards the registrar.
A number is stamped on his wrist.
He fingers the number.
This too has to be caressed.
This way, Sir . . .

Bowing like an acolyte
he takes the voting-paper
in both hands.
A stillness falls in the polling-station.

The old man Xs his paper,
folds it, holds it
over the ballot-box.

He cannot let it go.

Wild Goose

I want to tell you this:
The moment will surely come
when the Holy Spirit
will be within you –
a wild goose
stretching and straining
through storms
with her taut body
determined.

For that moment
there will be nothing dove
about the Spirit
as she fiercely leads you
through wholesome refusals
and undreamt of surrenders
out into those wonderfully clear choices
within the boundaries of which
you will land so awkwardly.
But you will be like her,
exhilarated in your every part
by such strong-winged
full-feathered
single-hearted
flight.

Bishop Tutu and Us

Bishop Tutu says
the sky is still up
in South Africa where
Blacks and Whites are walking
arm-in-arm in the streets.

Bishop Tutu says
the sky will still be up
in Northern Ireland
when Catholic and Protestant
live with one another
in ways undreamt of until now.

Tonight I take a leaf
from Bishop Tutu's book
on which to write a letter
which begins

My Love,
The sky will still be up
when you and I . . .

Saint Manchan and Pope Francis

Everywhere in Christendom
in churches decked in linen
in keeping with Saint Manchan's desire
you will find the open book
of the clean white scriptures
marked by the thumbage

of daily use and by ribbons
in all the colours of the rainbow.

Stained-glass light will fall
where you are sitting
peacefully at prayer, and still

in keeping with Pope Francis' desire
men and women everywhere
stricken by the message
of the clean white scriptures
will carry it out
to the streets, the city squares
to the noise, the uproar
and the mess of daily life.

Hurting from their work
they will return bruised and dirty
tiredly happy and content.

To a Young Man on the Street

This doorway your dwelling
this wall your gable
this railing your stairwell
this step your table.

This awning your shelter
this rain your window
this cupped coin your wages
this sunshine your shadow.

This streetlight your gatepost
this pavement your pathway
this corner your threshold
this cardboard your pillow.

This blanket your comfort
this night dream your meadow
this country your longing
this city your sorrow.

This hunger your waking
this traffic your morning
this held cup your asking
your loneliness throbbing.

Unbent

She was bent double
and quite unable to stand upright.

It's not for us to know her name
or what she was bent upon
for eighteen years
what was troubling her
in body or in soul
what doubled down her life
to the small arc of ground
around her feet.

In the synagogue that day
when Jesus called her up
to the full height of her body
and restored to her
the world she had missed

she felt forgotten
strength rising in her bones
running all the way back home
hoping they'd recognise her.

We know that Woman is her name.
We read her suffering
in daily headline news
from round the corner

of the world. She's waiting
at the synagogue to meet
that healing man again.
Eighteen years and counting.

Whose Miracle is This?

Some people came, bringing him
a paralytic, carried by four men.

Despite their blistered hands
four men undid a roof that day
to lower the paralyzed man
their friend, down in front of Jesus.
It was an easing precarious as birth.

They had carried him so long
cleared pathways
in every crowded town for him
down all the years, and now,

in an unexpected moment
they realised the freedom
of this miracle was theirs
as well as his. They shook
their aching shoulders out.

They had laid their burden down.

Rosary Woman

In a quiet place
the Rosary Woman
is fingering her beads
naming the mysteries
of a lifetime.

She has walked them
over and over
can tell their stories
as she has lived them

The Joyful
The Sorrowful
The Glorious

and as she prays she knows
there are new beads to count on
new mysteries to be named
and lived by her

The Possible
The Shocking
The Miraculous.

What to Drink

Not
the battered chalice
of the past

but the cup
of now
to sip

for nourishment.

A Visit
for Brigid

Every Mary needs an Elizabeth –
someone to confide in
when suddenly there's something
to be reckoned with.

Every Mary needs
a house that she can go to
hurriedly across the fields
where a door has been left open
as if for a visitor due to call.

All that Mary seeks in her Elizabeth
is good advice, or none. Perhaps
a conversation will suffice, because

Elizabeth will have such wisdom
of her own to share that Mary,
having visited an hour with her
may set out for home again
reciting as she goes the prayer

My soul magnifies the Lord.
My spirit rejoices in God my saviour
because the almighty
has done great things for me
and holy is God's name.

Notes

To Walk in my Native Place p.21.
This place is the townland of Cloonbaniff,
located between the villages of Lavagh and
Cloonacool, in south County Sligo.

Whin Honey p.27. Whin is also known as
gorse or furze.

Court Abbey p.46. A 15th century
Franciscan Friary, at Lavagh, County Sligo.

In Eidfjiord Norway p.51. A stave church is
a medieval wooden church common in
north western Europe.

Paradox p.55. Patrick Leigh Fermor
(1915-2011), British, wrote travel books
describing his walk across Europe in the
1930s.

Suffrage p.60. Sr. Dorrie Balfe, Dominican,
who had the role of observer in the first
free elections in S. Africa, in 1994, told me
the story of the man in this poem.

cont.

Saint Manchan and Pope Francis p.64.
This poem has some of the words and
images from the writings of both men: St.
Manchan's Prayer, a 10th century Irish
poem; Interview with Pope Francis,
conducted by Antonio Sparado SJ, Aug
2013, and The Joy of the Gospel by Pope
Francis, Veritas 2013, chapter 1.

Unbent p.66. Refers to the cure of the
woman bent double. Luke 13:10-13.

Whose Miracle is This? p.68. Refers to the
cure of the paralytic. Mark 2:1-12.

A Visit p.71. Refers to The Visitation.
Luke 1: 39-56.

All biblical quotes from The Jerusalem
Bible.